Once There Was A Tree

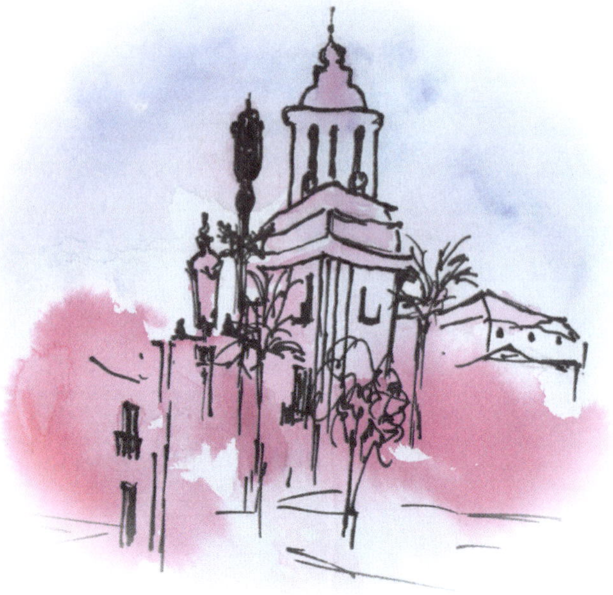

And on a night like this
the kind of night the living world
has never known before
when nothing makes the smallest noise
or moves in all this silent bliss
there are no eyes to see.....
the supernatural beauty of a night like this..
the trees stand still
as if waiting for a kiss
from just a breath of wind
but the night stands still.....

If there is an enemy
that walks the night
he is invisible
and fear was never greater
no faces at the windows
no eyes look down
on a night like this...
and the old familiar square
is alien now
on a night like this.....

# Once There Was A Tree

by

dorina

Text copyright © Dorina Gutherless
Artwork copyright © Dorina Gutherless
ISBN: 9798842396160
Book design Maritza Garvie

## The Beginning......

There was curfew – a time to go out and a time to be home again – time to go shopping and always alone and time to take out the rubbish..

Just the necessary things were the only reason for being allowed to leave the house..

I began to go a little further each day with my bag of rubbish and that's when I met the tree..

At first she was a landmark, steadfast, serene and as strong as she was gentle. I felt her kindness and soft touch of her leaves as if she was saying 'Hello'.

Then I began to wander even further – to 'dangerous places I was told that were unsafe to walk to'. But I never felt unsafe – once I was almost lost and a kind girl with her dog put me back on my tracks and I was home by eleven PM - just in time and still with my bag of rubbish.

Sometimes I would see people out on their own like me and there would always be some kind of 'Hello' or eye to eye experience and every day a little picture would appear on paper.

The paper itself was hard to find as all the shops had sold all their drawing paper to parents of children needing to pass the long hours of no school. It was in an old shop at the back of town where I was able to buy very old paper off an old shelf but this old fragile paper lent itself beautifully to colour.

That was – in its own way – the beginning ..

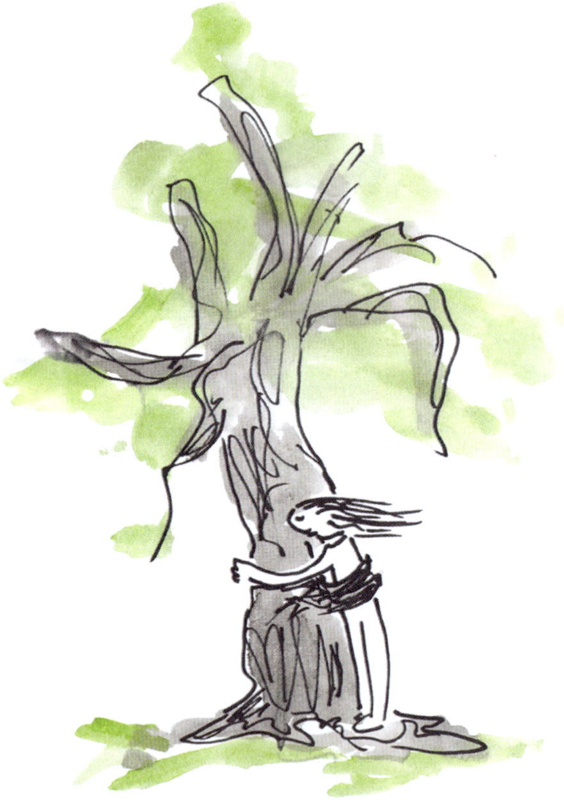

Once there was a tree .. and lockdown ..
and just me and a little bag of rubbish ..
but there was the tree...

You hold me tight
I am light and small
I can reach high and grow tall
I smell all your springtime ,,
One can only hear what one can hear,
see what one can see ..
And feel?
"I feel the magic in the air tonight" said the tree ..
"And that's alright by me" ..

You hold tight ..

Holding close ... heart on heart ..
sharing secrets ...

No words to say tree,
just sitting here with you is enough

Baby Blackbirds going 'Cheep, cheep, cheep',
do you know that one day
you will sing the sweetest, purest song?
And I, too, have many, many songs to sing ..

Quiet moments and the little things - always there - just the little things ..

"How ever did I get so high
and how far would I see from here, tree?'
'That one never knows
but you're here now
and safe with me.
"I love your dress, your young beauty ..
like the colours I would wear in springtime
before I got to be so old."

Suspended and safe.
The friendliness of the old tree ..

People you meet  - things you find.
Just a little happiness along the way -
that's all....

The energy giving tree ..
feeling good ..

The thinking tree where - for just a little while -
things at odds come together
and dark becomes light and soft again..
The tree can feel, can hear - can even shed a tear ...

At the end of the day, quiet moments are the best..'
Yes', said the tree - 'they are'....

Lonely hearts .. Careless love...

We're all here....branches touching .. clinking glasses,
horses are happy ..
One of those moments ..

Across the railway line
there's just a hut
and hills behind where the sun goes down.
There's a goat
and chickens, too..
A simple life without a care
a song to sing which fills the air
the little things
and a tune to play
for the girl who sings
that's all..

The day is done ..

Little old house ... kind old tree ...
a bit of love..

Always colour - and a cat - or two..

Blue sky dreams
Blue door fantasies
Blue, blue dreams ..
Dreams into two
Goes two into dreams
And blue – just blue ..

Blue ..

Hearts don't break - they only ache - sometimes forever..

The Gathering Heart...

Nobody must ever forget how to love ..

Back to the old tree - for a while -

another story-

There are so many to tell ..

Perfect little house,
perfect little street,
blue flowers around the door..
'Morning Glory', she said
so here am I..
'What will happen if I knock on the door?'
'what will happen if you don't?'

Knock knock ..

El Querido - and the old tango playing, it was
like the first time and that seems so long ago.
How the mind wanders and remembers!
How patient are the trees..

El Querido .. listening to music ..
Paco de Lucia

Into the dark night
and silent street
goes the lone guitarist.
Curfew calls him home
and only the trees
and the little magic people
can hear the songs
and music floating in the air ..

Curfew calling ..

No words to say, tree – just sitting here with you is enough..
you are your own memory ..
you are the dream ..

Everybody has a story to tell ..

Earth changing colours
bright autumn skies, red and gold leaves
and beauty.
We can't see eye-to-eye
you and I, little fox ..
If I look at you, you run away ..
Like you, I hold my breath, stay still
and we share this moment ..

you and I, little fox ..

Carefree moments sometimes are the best
and the warmth of the listening heart..

Back to the wind, face to the wind,
letting go .. holding tight ...

In the silence of night
out of a starry sky
one star falls
and there we are
- just tree and I
and tree holds me tight ..

as I hold the star ..

End of the day time.
Colours of the sun
and early rising moon ..
grass bright green and earth still wet from rain.
Spirits of the earth at play...

In the silence of night - out of a starry sky -
one star falls - and there we are -
just tree and I ..

Only for a moment I knock upon your door ..
once more ..
just once more  ..
2020

A door opens and here we come again…
a new star shines above ..
her name is Hope ..

The end of the season ..
some of us have to leave ..
it's a time to move on ..
they cannot choose to stay..
But it's sad to see them go..'
Don't forget us', said the trees

But it's sad to see them go ..

Out on a limb – shifting between light and shade -
and in my wanderings,
I find the tree..

Two eyes.. one for love and the here and now ...
The other for the changing heart..
and what might have been..

Another wild windy day – feeling blue but there's always you, tree ..
and so I hang on ..

"Hide and you shall seek .. lose and you shall find -
whichever way, the story will tell itself",
said the tree ..

"Don't cry!" said the tree ..
"The sun is setting  - beauty is everywhere.
Sometimes you only have to let your eyes see it."

The kiss as the sun goes down ...

Lost in isolation
finding inspiration
feeling unseen
and held
in this lovely place ..
Space
and music for the mind
to swirl around in ..
this is the best of trees
trust ..
and a place to hide ..

When the tree listens ..

The innocence of springtime ..

Behind the wall is a tree and behind that is another tree.
Beyond is a pink sky. Nothing moves and all is silence,
I sit and think  - don't ask me what  -
you don't want to know ..

My horse and I ...
our friend the tree
and the sweet grass around..

How far can I go? How far can you see?

Is this the final curatin
or is it just for now
I take a bow?
Before I go again,
wearing blue for you again ,
to dance
again ..

Blue again ..

Printed in Great Britain
by Amazon